Your Journey to Financial Wellness *Achieve Success* is a well- written LIF advice as well as clear instructions. . I will refer to for years to come. Appli the lifeblood of our lifestyles, and th ~~~~~~~~~~~~~~ ~~~~~~~ I felt like I was getting valuable tips from my fun, respected friend.

Ebony M. Hines
Independent Life Insurance Agent
Indianapolis, IN

Jethella Nolan Young has laid out a blueprint for financial freedom and peace of mind. This book is not only for the younger generation looking to purchase a home or car but also for people planning on early retirement or those who will be retiring in a few years. Do not automatically think this is going to be hard or that you don't have the time to do this. How do you know until you try? My father always said, "Nothing beats a failure but a try." Be the person who will try to climb that ladder to success and peace of mind. This book will help you get there. When you look back, you will tell yourself, "I made it!"

Greta Wingfield
Retired Legal Administrative Assistant
Chicago, IL

I feel like most people don't have a clue about handling their finances. People need to ask themselves whether the item they are purchasing is a need or want. **Your Journey to Financial Wellness: A Simple Guide to Help You Achieve Success** *will help you to set realistic goals and expectations for what you want in life. It is a blueprint for managing your money, staying out of debt, building wealth, and maintaining a good credit score! Jethella did a great job of giving a step-by-step approach to building wealth and eliminating debt! I love it!*

S.J.
Educational Professional
Chicago, IL

Your Journey to
FINANCIAL WELLNESS

A Simple Guide to Help You Achieve Success

JETHELLA NOLAN-YOUNG

KishKnows
PUBLISHING

Your Journey to Financial Wellness:
A Simple Guide to Help You Achieve Success
by Jethella Nolan-Young

Cover design, editing, book layout, and publishing services by KishKnows, Inc., Richton Park, Illinois, 708-252-DOIT admin@kishknows.com, www.kishknows.com

ISBN: 978-0-578-99368-3
LCCN: 2021920640

Special Dedication

This book is dedicated to everyone who believed in me and encouraged me to follow my dream; especially my husband, who has been a true inspiration and always knows what to say.

A special thanks to my prayer warriors—because we know God *does* answer prayers. Please enjoy your financial journey!

Table of Contents

Preface   i

Chapter 1: Financial Goals   1

Chapter 2: Debt Management Skills   7

Chapter 3: Understanding Credit Scores   15

Chapter 4: Credit Reporting   21

Chapter 5: Credit Repair Tips   25

A Final Message: Where Do I Go from Here?   31

Resources   32

About the Author   33

Contact the Author   34

Preface

My first spending workshop was held at my church in Alabama over twenty years ago. Some of our church members were unable to take care of necessary expenses and begin saving to purchase homes. My pastor approached me, and we briefly discussed his concern. I agreed to facilitate a meeting that would help; and after I completed some research, the meeting became a workshop which focused on poor spending habits. It was an intimate group, and I wanted to take a hands-on approach.

The workshops were well received by our church members, and many members began saving money, purchasing homes, and building wealth. Some of the members shared what they learned with their children and provided updates and positive feedback.

As a young adult, it seemed I was always helping my family and friends with financial issues by lending or giving them money. I decided to stop handing out money every time someone called me in tears, and instead began helping them to manage their poor spending habits. Occasionally, I would loan money to a family member or friend; but when I did, I would invite them to a workshop because my goal was to make a lifelong impact on their finances. I was not always successful, but I kept trying. If they refused to attend the workshop, I put an end to the monetary gifts. It was a hard position to take; however, it was needed to help them learn to make better financial choices.

Several years ago, I was discussing credit scores with a dear friend, and I realized that there was no reason why I should not strive for an excellent credit score. I began researching the process and committed myself to one day making it happen. Today, my credit score is 827, which is the highest it has ever been in my life.

In this book, I want to share everything that I have learned over the years with both my workshop attendees and my readers. An excellent credit score will open doors that some of us never realized were closed.

Financial wellness begins with the choices we make. Let us begin to make better financial choices.

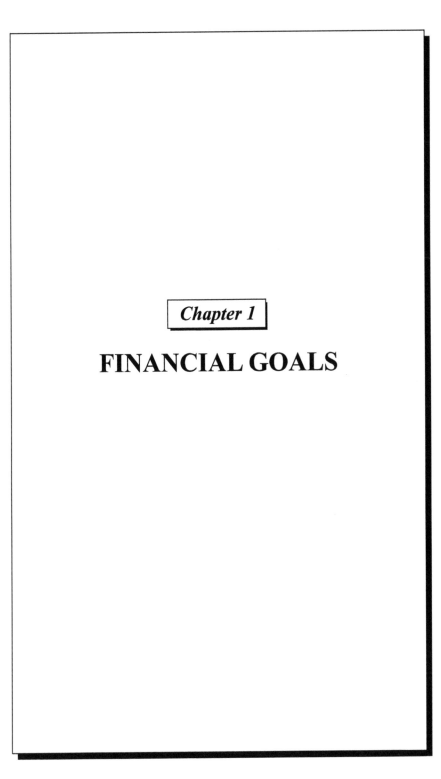

Chapter 1

FINANCIAL GOALS

Why Do I Need Financial Goals?

You may be someone who has never set a goal and may not understand the purpose behind goal-setting. A goal is *an idea or a result that you plan and commit to achieving within a specific time frame.* If you are trying to advance in your career or accomplish certain things in your life, goals help you to stay focused, which helps to minimize distractions.

I try to set goals that include spiritual, personal, and financial aspects. I make sure my goals are set on January 1st and commit to writing them down. Life has taught me that writing my goals down helps me to hold myself accountable—and my chances of success skyrocket. Please try this, and begin to measure your success.

I position my goals in a location where I can see them daily. At first, I posted them on the refrigerator; but after a while, I started placing them inside my computer cabinet. I make revisions and updates as needed throughout the year.

Always set *clear, effective, specific,* and *realistic* goals. If you fall short when it comes to holding yourself accountable, share your goals with a loved one or someone you trust, and have them help you.

If you are new to goal-setting, you may not be familiar with SMART goals. SMART is an acronym that stands for *Specific, Measurable, Achievable, Realistic,* and *Timely.* A SMART goal incorporates these criteria to increase your chances of success.

- Specific: What exactly are you going to do?

- Measurable: You need to be able to track your progress. Think, "How much?" or "How many?".

- **A**chievable: Be realistic; losing ten pounds in four months is possible, losing ten pounds in four days is not.

- **R**elevant: Your goal should be important to you.

- **T**ime-Based: When do you want to accomplish your goal? *Always* set a date.

For years, I struggled with completing personal goals successfully. Work-related goals were not a problem, but I always put my personal goals on the back burner. My personal goals were important to me, but my plate was always too full, so there was not enough time in my day to get to them. I had to learn how to prioritize my personal growth, and setting goals helped me to do that. I used the SMART strategy because it was important to me that I accomplish my goals.

There were times when I set goals that I knew would be difficult to achieve. I called them my "stretch goals." At the beginning of the year, I would set multiple goals, but only one stretch goal. Managing stress was always a personal goal, and setting one stretch goal helped me manage my stress level. Sometimes, I was hard on myself; but accomplishing my goals was a priority, and I needed positive results.

Let me give you an example of one of my personal financial goals. I wanted to purchase my first home by the age of thirty-one. I knew I had to start by increasing my understanding of homeownership. In 1986, when I first set my goals for purchasing my own home, they looked something like this:

- **S**pecific: Purchase a home in a safe area with a good public school system.

- **M**easurable: Begin saving $300 each month.

- **A**chievable: Purchase the home by August 1989.

- **R**elevant: I want my son to grow up in his own home.

- **T**ime-based: I am determined to purchase my own home before I turn thirty-one in August 1989.

When I look back on that time in my life, my dedication to accomplishing my goals is evident. I moved into my home during the summer of 1989, just in time for my son to begin school in a new district.

Goal setting can be powerful, but if we choose not to put any action to the goals we set, they are only words on a piece of paper. You will discover that you become a better person as you begin achieving your goals. You cannot allow anything or anyone to get in your way or supply negative energy that may hinder you from achieving them. Think about the "Three Ds" when setting your goals:

| **Dedication** | **Determination** | **Discipline** |

You should always think about where *you are today* and have an idea of *where you want to go*. That may sound difficult, but it is really very simple. You should always want to *achieve* more, *accomplish* more, and *be* more. Take some time to evaluate your situation. You need a little quiet time to think about where you are and where you want to go. This is not something you can get from a friend or a sibling because the answer is within you alone.

Take a few minutes and write down your top three financial goals. I have learned never to write more than three goals at a time. There may be several things you want to accomplish; however, focus on a few. As soon as you achieve one of your goals, remove it from the list and add another one. You must be careful not to let yourself get overwhelmed because you need to stay in control of the process.

One of your goals should be to experience financial wellness. You need overall good financial health and well-being. Start by jotting down three goals here. Don't overthink it right now—you can go back and revise them later.

1.

2.

3.

After you have set *clear, effective, specific,* and *realistic* goals, then you can write out an action plan. It can be intimidating, but remember to keep things simple. You need to put a plan in place to help you achieve your goals.

You are going to hear this statement throughout this book: KEEP IT SIMPLE.

Here is an example of a SIMPLE action plan format:

Action Step	Responsibilities	Timeline	Resources
What will be done?	Who will perform the action?	By when?	-Available -Needed
Item 1:			
Item 2:			
Item 3:			

You may want to complete the action steps for each financial goal. Please, *please* do not overthink this process.

Keep track of your success. You need to know when you are making progress, and you need to measure your progress. You need to know when your goal has been reached because this can be the time to set additional goals.

Chapter 2

DEBT MANAGEMENT
SKILLS

How did I get here?

Too often, we find ourselves in more debt than we can manage. Too much debt is often the result of poor spending habits. We make purchases to impress others or satisfy some inner desire to possess unnecessary things. I have friends who have purchased clothing that they never wore. At the time of the purchase, they felt they could not live without those items; however, after they were placed in their closets, something changed. You may have asked yourself one of the following questions at one time or another:

- Why did I purchase these shoes?

- I have seven pairs of black slacks...why did I buy another pair?

- I bought this dress for a special occasion and only wore it once. Why?

It can be so easy to get into debt; however, it can take *years* to dig ourselves out of the hole. The most important thing you need to learn is this: Once you decide to get out of debt, *you must not create any new debt*. I struggled with this personally, and my own journey to financial wellness took commitment.

If you manage the household finances, make sure everyone in the house is involved. The household should share the same *financial vision*. We cannot have one family member managing their spending well while another family member is spending every dime they touch.

There may come a time when an adult member of the household needs to receive an allowance. If someone in your household refuses or is unable to manage their finances, someone needs to take control and manage the money that said family member is allowed to spend.

Remember, the end goal is financial wellness for the entire family...and you *can* get there. As you move closer to the end goal, sit back and watch your credit score increase.

At this moment, our focus is managing our debt, and we need to commit ourselves to not creating any more. Please consider not using your credit cards during this time. If you do not have the cash, do not make the purchase. By doing so, you will become less dependent on your credit cards.

One way to help manage your debt is to begin managing your spending. Some of us may have good spending habits; however, many of us have work to do. If you need help, I suggest you complete a thirty-day spending exercise.

Spending Exercise

Track your spending for thirty days. This will help you identify any waste. I provide my workshop attendees with a small notebook to help simplify this process, but you can use anything to record this data. You must record everything you spend—*no exceptions*. The waste you identify in your daily spending should be used later to eliminate your debt. Some of your waste may look like the following:

- Eating out excessively.

- Buying expensive morning coffee.

- Paying full price for items that will go on sale
  (and everything goes on sale eventually).

- Not using coupons and a list when you go grocery shopping.

While doing this exercise, you must be honest with yourself because you are the one who will benefit. Initially, this may seem tedious; but remember, this will help you get closer to the end goal.

After you identify the waste in your spending, you must make conscious and deliberate choices NOT to spend money on those items anymore and to not waste that money on some other frivolous purchases.

Monthly Budget

Do you have a weekly or monthly budget? If the answer is no, *please* begin operating your household within a budget. Getting started may be challenging; however, you need to spend the time creating your budget now. You need to know what is coming in and what is going out of the household. If you are paid weekly, you may want to set up a weekly budget. On the other hand, I have found a monthly budget works best for most households because most bills are paid monthly.

You can use a spreadsheet, notebook, or whatever method works for you. You can even go online and find budget forms with the formulas already in the document. We are going to talk about your budget in more detail later.

A few tips for setting a personal budget:

- Keep it simple.

- Set a time frame.

- Build your emergency fund into your budget.

- Do not worry about the perfect record keeping method.

- Make sure everyone in the household is involved and on the same page.

- Make adjustments, as needed.

- Do not set yourself up for failure.

You must record your monthly income, including wages, salaries, commissions, tips, bonuses, dividends, Social Security payments, and pensions.

Always record everything going out, which includes things like tithes and offerings, rent or mortgage, utilities, groceries, life insurance, car insurance, student loans, credit card payments, personal loans, contributions to your emergency fund, and investments.

Here are some examples of additional data you may have on your document:

- Name of creditor/lender
- Monthly payment
- Due date
- Debt elimination
- Annual Percentage Rate (APR)
- Debt utilization percentage

I cannot say this enough: once you have taken the time to create a household budget, *use it.*

Elimination of Debt

Many of us struggle to get out of debt. One of the biggest reasons we struggle is we *continue creating debt.* I know I said this earlier, but I need you to understand how to *stop* creating debt. Eliminating debt requires discipline and commitment. Before you begin this journey, you must decide that financial wellness is what you really want. Getting started is not easy; however, you need to understand that achieving the end goal is rewarding.

It is time for you to begin eliminating your debt, and I am going to share a method that has worked for many of my clients. I tried this method for the first time over twenty years ago, and it still works today. This method will eliminate debt and improve your debt utilization, which has an immediate impact on your credit score.

You need to calculate your utilization on each credit card. Divide the outstanding balance on the credit card by the credit limit to arrive at the utilization percentage.

Credit Card Utilization Example

The outstanding balance on XYZ credit card is $2,500, and the credit card limit is $5,000. Divide 2,500 by 5,000 and you will see that the credit card utilization is 50%. Complete this exercise for each of your credit cards.

When you start eliminating debt, focus on paying the credit cards with the highest utilization first. This is because 30% of your credit score is based on credit card utilization. List your credit cards in descending order starting with the highest utilization. You can list the highest credit card as "A," the second highest as "B," and the third highest as "C." Continue through the alphabet, as needed, until all credit cards are listed. Remember, paying off debt should follow a systematic fashion; it gives you the biggest bang for your buck.

Once you place your credit card debts in descending order, it is time to begin eliminating them. You should always pay more than the minimum payment required on each credit card. You might be thinking, "I barely have the minimum and you want me to pay more?" Yes! If you want to get out of debt, it is time to make sacrifices.

If you completed the spending exercise, you likely found some waste in your spending and need to put that money to use, and pay off some debt. You can start small because every penny counts. If you have stopped eating out as often and buying expensive coffee, put those dollars in an envelope, and use that money to pay down the credit card you identified as "A" on your list. Every time you receive additional income, which may come from a bonus, commission, tip, or wage/salary, apply that extra money to the creditor you identified as "A" on your list.

As soon as you pay off Creditor A on your list, focus on the next one. The money you were paying Creditor A is already in your budget; therefore, *do not think you have extra money to spend.* Add the money that you were paying Creditor A to the money you are currently paying the creditor you identified as Creditor B on your list. After you pay off Creditor B, you are going to move that money to help pay off Creditor C. Do you see the process? It is simple, but it only works if you put it into action.

Please understand...*this will take time.* Stay focused, and you will eliminate your consumer debt.

If your credit card utilization is not out of control, you should pay off your credit card with the highest interest rate first. You always want to keep your interest rate to a minimum because interest is the money you are paying the lender in order to use their money.

This is a very simple financial concept, and I don't want you to overthink this process. Keep it simple, and stay away from high interest rates. There is no value in paying these.

We may carry consumer debt from time to time, but the debt we carry should be healthy. As soon as your debt becomes too large for you to manage comfortably, it is no longer healthy.

After you have erased your consumer debt and created your emergency fund, you can start investing and building wealth. Please consult with a financial advisor to determine what investments will work best for you and your family.

Chapter 3

UNDERSTANDING YOUR CREDIT SCORE

I have always had a good credit score. I purchased my first new car without a cosigner when I was nineteen. At that time, I didn't really understand credit scores. After graduating from college, I received several preapproved credit card applications. I fell into what I thought was a glamorous lifestyle. I had a purse full of credit cards and was paying the minimum monthly payments. This went on for a few years until I decided to purchase a home before my thirty-first birthday.

I set a goal and was determined to achieve it. I improved my understanding of homeownership, including the financial requirements. I knew I wanted a good interest rate and researched how to make it happen. My time was spent reading finance articles and listening to financial professionals.

While doing my research, I began to understand the importance of a good credit score and how it is calculated. I was committed to having an excellent credit score, but it was not easy. I was determined and stayed the course, and my score began to improve. I had no one in my immediate circle who understood my drive to obtain an excellent credit score. Because of this, I was a bit apprehensive about sharing my financial experience with anyone.

Now that I have an excellent credit score, I want to help others achieve that milestone. I am going to share some information to help you understand how credit scores are calculated.

What is a credit score and why should I care about it?

Credit scoring is *a statistical analysis performed by lenders and financial institutions to assess a person's creditworthiness.* Lenders use credit scores, among other things, to decide whether to extend credit. A person's credit score is a number between 300 and 850, with 850 being the highest credit rating possible.

Potential employers may ask you to authorize a background screening as part of the application process. This screening may include checking your credit report. Employers are most likely to check credit when the job requires you to manage finances or handle sensitive data.

Insurance companies also have a scoring system to help determine the risk of a potential customer. Did you know you also have an insurance score? This is something else for you to think about. There are lots of analytical databases that calculate insurance scores. Insurance companies analyze how you handled finances and insurance in the past. They compare those traits to policyholders who had claims to determine the likelihood that you will have a claim. The bigger the "risk" they consider you to be, the higher the premium will be for your policy.

There is a difference between a credit score and an insurance score. A credit score is used by *banks, credit card companies,* and *lenders* to measure their confidence in your ability to repay a loan or debt. They consider things like your debt-to-income ratio, payment history, and job history.

An insurance score is more about how you *interact* with your financial accounts versus what is in them. The insurance score considers things like:

- Have you held your accounts steady for a long period of time?

- Did you make your payments on time?

- How often did you reach your credit limit?

Improving your credit score can also improve your insurance score.

How is your credit score calculated?

35%: Payment History

Your *payment history* carries the most weight when calculating your credit score. On-time payments indicate whether you will make payments on time in the future, which is extremely important to lenders. Too often, we have the money needed to pay a creditor, and we spend that money on something we think is more important. Please remember: you *made* the debt, and you need to be responsible and *pay* the debt.

Many years ago, I registered with an online service that helps me track my credit score. I received an email a few weeks ago congratulating me for 152 months of on-time payments. That is *twelve-and-a-half years* of on-time payments since I began tracking my credit score. That takes discipline, and you can make that happen in your life too.

30%: Credit Limit Usage

Lenders look for signs of responsible usage. The *less* you use your available credit, the *better* your credit score. As a simple example, let's say you receive a credit card with a $5,000 limit, and the first thing you want to do is go out and use the credit card. Always keep the amount you owe less than 30%. If your credit limit is $5,000, the amount you charge on the card should never exceed $1,500.

It takes discipline, but you got this!

15%: Length of Credit History

The age of your oldest account is an indication of how much experience you have handling credit. This is why it is important not to close accounts. You may have to use the credit card periodically to keep the account open. You can make a small purchase—just remember to pay the balance in full before the due date. I have clients who pay their mobile phone bills every month on a credit card to keep the account open. This method helps improve your payment history, credit limit usage, and the length of credit history.

10%: Credit Mix

The credit mix tells lenders that you can manage a variety of credit. Types of credit can include a mortgage, an installment loan, revolving credit (department store credit cards are a good example of this), and an auto loan, to name a few.

10%: New Credit

Lenders pay attention to how often and when you decide to open new accounts. Opening too many new accounts in a short window of time could point to credit problems. Always remember: lenders are assessing your *risk* and your *ability to pay your debt.*

Chapter 4

CREDIT REPORTING

What is credit reporting?

A credit report is *a list of your present and past credit accounts and loans which are reported by businesses and financial institutions with whom you have done business.* Those businesses and financial institutions may report your credit and loan history to one or more of the major credit reporting agencies. The three major credit reporting agencies are Equifax, Experian, and TransUnion.

Most businesses and financial institutions don't report to all three major credit reporting agencies, and lenders report data to the credit reporting agencies at different times of the month. This may result in one agency having more up-to-date information than another agency. The credit reporting agencies may record, store, or display the same information differently.

You need to understand what information is included on your credit report. It includes identifying information, such as your name and Social Security number, your credit cards and loan details (open and closed), how much money you owe, and whether you pay your bills on time.

Not all of your consumer payment history is included in a credit report. For example, my new cellphone provider checked my credit report before making the decision to provide service; however, they did not report my monthly on-time payments to the credit reporting agencies.

Your credit *report* and your credit *score* are not the same thing. A credit score mathematically represents the information that is compiled in your credit report. It can range from 300 to 850, with 850 being excellent. *Always strive for excellence.* As stated earlier, a credit report is a list of your present and past credit accounts and loans, which are reported by businesses and financial institutions with whom you have done business.

Lenders use credit scores when setting interest rates. When you are applying for credit, you may receive a lower interest rate when you have a higher credit score; so maintaining a high credit score will save you a lot of money. I mentioned in the previous chapter that you need to keep your interest rates as low as possible. Remember, *interest is the money you pay a lender/creditor for using their money*. A high interest rate has no value to you as a consumer. The lower the interest rate, the lower your payments. You should never want something so badly that you will pay any interest rate. The less interest you pay, the better for you because that means *more money stays in your pocket*.

A few major takeaways:

1. Lenders use credit reports to determine your ability to repay a debt.

2. Credit reports show your history of making on-time payments and the risk you present taking on new debt.

3. Understanding your credit report enables you to improve your credit score.

You can request a copy of your credit report anytime. The Fair and Accurate Credit Transactions Act, passed in 2003, entitles you to one free credit report every year from each of the three main credit bureaus. The contact information for each of the major credit bureaus is listed in the Resources section at the end of the book.

Things to know about credit reporting:

The credit reporting time limit is *the maximum amount of time credit bureaus can include delinquent debts on your credit report*. For most types of accounts, it is seven years from the date of delinquency. Bankruptcies are reported for ten years, and tax liens can be reported for up to fifteen years.

The credit reporting time limit is dictated by the Fair Credit Reporting Act and does not influence the statute of limitations (the period of time that a debt is legally enforceable) for collecting a debt. The time period starts on the account's last date of activity, depending upon the type of debt you have. This varies by state. The statute of limitations is usually between three and six years but can be as long as ten to fifteen years in some states.

Debt falls into one of four categories. It is important to know which type of debt you have because the time limits are different for each.

    a. **Oral Agreements** are *debts made in an oral contract.* With an oral contract, you only made a verbal agreement to pay back the loan. Nothing was put in writing.

    b. **Written Contracts** are *debts with a contract signed by you and the creditor.* A contract includes terms and conditions of the loan, i.e., the amount of the loan and monthly payment.

    c. A **Promissory Note** is a *written agreement to pay back a debt in certain payments, at a certain interest rate, and by a certain date and time.* Mortgages and student loans are types of promissory notes.

    d. **Open-Ended Account** is *an account with a revolving balance that you can repay and borrow on again.* Credit cards, in-store credit, and lines of credit are open-ended accounts.

You can ask an attorney if you have questions about which type of debt you have.

Chapter 5

CREDIT REPAIR
TIPS

Should I pay someone to repair my credit?

Credit repair agencies can be very costly. Before you make the decision to pay someone to fix your credit, consider doing it yourself. Start by reviewing your most recent credit report from each agency for accuracy. If you find discrepancies, dispute them immediately. (You will get more information to help you dispute errors later in this chapter.)

Credit Inquiries

A credit inquiry is *a request made by a lender for credit report information from a credit-reporting agency*. Every time you apply for any form of credit and provide your Social Security number, you give the lender permission to view your credit report. Inquiries are classified as either a "hard inquiry" or a "soft inquiry."

A *hard inquiry* is a type of credit information request that includes your full credit report. Hard inquiries are normally used for credit approvals and some background checks. Hard inquiries can negatively impact your credit score.

A *soft inquiry* happens when a lender or credit card company checks your credit to preapprove you for an offer. An insurance provider may also perform a soft inquiry. Soft inquiries do not impact your credit score because they are not attached to a specific credit application.

Limit your inquiries because lenders view too many inquiries as a sign of risk. Inquiries stay on your credit report for two years. Please use the following chart as a guideline for inquiries within two years.

TOTAL INQUIRIES	RATING
0	EXCELLENT
1 - 2	GOOD
3 - 5	AVERAGE
>5	FAIR

e-Oscar

e-Oscar is a web-based, automated system that enables credit reporting agencies to create and respond to consumer credit history disputes. e-Oscar scans your letter of dispute and responds to the credit agency with a code used to address your dispute. Since it is an automated system, mistakes can happen during the verification process. For this reason, you may want to consider writing your dispute letters by hand. When you handwrite your letter, it will be automatically rejected, which will result in a human being researching your dispute.

Credit Disputing Strategy

Under the Fair Credit Reporting Act, the dispute should be sent to the credit bureaus. You can only dispute errors. You cannot dispute accurate information on your credit report and expect the credit bureaus to remove the information; however, you *can* hold the credit bureaus liable under the Fair Credit Reporting Act if they fail to observe the time limit on your debt.

Debt collectors often sell accounts to one another; and sometimes, the debt collectors will report inaccurate timelines. Those inaccurate timelines may cause debt to be reported longer than it should. This process is known as the "re-aging" of debt. Under the Fair Credit Reporting Act, this should not happen, and you have the right to dispute this inaccurate information.

Please remember the following tips:

- Always send detailed, handwritten letters when disputing information.

- Include specific details explaining why the information reported is incorrect.

- Include evidence proving the mistake.

I mentioned writing letters because I may be old school when it comes to communication. Many of you would rather dispute electronically—please remember that you need supporting documents, and *you need to upload them*. Too often, when things get complicated, we walk away and never complete the process.

Keep it simple, and follow the process that works best for you. Your credit is important, and *you should never walk away from repairing your credit*. One of your financial goals should be to improve your credit score, and if there are errors on your credit report, following this process is key.

If you are unsuccessful, you can file a complaint with the Consumer Financial Protection Bureau.

How to Dispute Items on a Credit Report

1. Write a letter to each reporting credit bureau.

2. Mail the letter using certified mail, "return receipt requested."

3. Wait at least thirty days before making inquiries into the status of your dispute. (The credit reporting agencies are obligated to investigate the matter within thirty days unless they somehow show your dispute to be frivolous.)

4. If applicable, ask the credit reporting agency to send notices of your revised credit report to any person or institution that received your credit report in the last six months.

5. The credit reporting agency must also send copies of the revised credit report to any person or institution that received your credit report in the last two years for purposes of employment.

6. If you do not receive a response to your inquiry within forty-five days or the incorrect item remains on your credit report, send another certified letter.

7. This time, mention that your rights under the Fair Credit Reporting Act (FCRA) were violated by the credit bureau's failure to promptly investigate and respond to your dispute.

8. Ask that a statement regarding the dispute be included in future reports if the investigation does not resolve the dispute.

Sample Credit Dispute Letter

(**Always**, *always* handwrite your letters!)

Date
Your Name
Your Address, City, State, Zip Code

Via Certified Mail #
Name of Credit Reporting Agency
Company Address
City, State, Zip Code

To Whom It May Concern:

I am writing to dispute incorrect information currently listed on my credit report. I have circled the item on the attached copy of the credit report. This item (include detailed information, i.e., name of source, such as creditors or tax court, and identify the type of item, such as credit account, judgment, etc.) is (inaccurate or incomplete) because (describe what is inaccurate or incomplete and why).

I am requesting that the item be removed (or request another specific change) to correct the information. Enclosed are copies of (describe any enclosed documentation, such as payment records or court documents) which support my dispute.

Please investigate this matter and (delete or correct) this disputed item immediately.

Sincerely,

Your name
Enclosures: (List what you are enclosing.)

A Final Message:

Where do I go from here?

I pray you have received an insight, credit repair tip, or debt management suggestion that will help you think about money differently.

- Did you take time to compile financial goals?

- Did you complete a thirty-day spending exercise to help you eliminate wasteful spending?

- Did you develop a monthly budget?

- Did you take the first step to eliminate debt?

- Do you have a better understanding of your credit scores?

- Now that you know how credit scores are calculated, will you pay your bills on time?

Your Journey to Financial Wellness is a simple guide that will help you make a big difference with your personal and business finances. You need to get started and make it happen!

It is very **SIMPLE!**

Resources

Credit Bureau Contact Information

Equifax Credit Information Services

Request credit report	P.O. Box 740241 Atlanta, GA 30374-0241 800-685-1111
Fraud Alert	Equifax.com or 888-766-0008

Experian

Request credit report	Experian.com 888-397-3742
Disputes	P.O. Box 4500 Allen, TX 75013

TransUnion

Request credit report	P.O. Box 1000 Chester, PA 19022 800-888-4213

About the Author

Jethella Nolan-Young is a graduate of the Kellogg School of Management, Northwestern University, with concentrations in Marketing and Management Policy. She spent many years with large and small organizations completing a multitude of assignments successfully.

Jethella's true passion was entrepreneurship, and she purchased *The Country's Best Yogurt* (TCBY) franchise in Eastpoint, Michigan. After years of positive return, she sold her franchise and spent a few years in education. Eventually, she returned to entrepreneurship and founded Alpha Omega Money Management, NFP. She retired from corporate America and shifted her focus instead to continue building Alpha Omega Money Management, NFP.

Jethella's goal was to educate disadvantaged communities with the skills needed to become self-sufficient. She conducted workshops in faith-based organizations, homeless shelters, and libraries. She wanted her audience to understand debt management skills, credit scores, tips to repair their own credit, and build wealth. Jethella recognized these needs and took action.

Jethella thanks God every day for how He is using her and for helping her to identify her purpose. Her first spending workshops were held in her church, and she continues to facilitate workshops within the church community.

She believes that we need to be good stewards, and we need to manage everything that God has entrusted to us...no questions asked.

Contact the Author

If you would like to contact the author, you may do so at:

Email:
aommanagement@yahoo.com

Website:
http://www.aommanagement.com